How

Master Your

Confidence

And Your Courage

By Paul Booth

Dedication

I dedicate this book to you the reader. Your willingness to master your confidence and master your courage tells me that you want more out of life. Being confident and courageous despite the difficulties life throws at us is indeed a challenge, but you are now meeting that challenge, as you implement the instructions in this book.

Thanks

My thanks go to Adriana Silvas whose help and support has made this book possible.

The measure of intelligence is the ability to change. Albert Einstein

Self-confidence is the foundation of all great success and achievement. Brian Tracy

The mind is everything. We are changed by our thoughts. What you think you become. Buddha

With confidence, you have won before you have started. Marcus Garvey

Yesterday I was clever, so I wanted to change the world. Today I am wise, so I am changing myself. Rumi

You will never do anything in this world without courage. It is the greatest quality of the mind, next to honour. Aristotle

Your mind only responds to two things: the pictures you make in your head and the words you say to yourself. And they are very easy to change. Marisa Peer

He who is not courageous enough to take risks, will accomplish nothing in life. Muhammad Ali

This Mastery Series

My intention is to publish at least 8 books in this Mastery Series. This is the second one in the series. The first one was, *How to Conquer Anxiety, Worry, Fear and Stress.* Still to come... *3) How to Master Your Self-Esteem, Self-Control & Responsibility. 4) How to Master Your Relationships. 5) How to Master Your Happiness. 6) How to Master Your Past, Present and Future. 7) How to Master Yourself and Your Life: Smile, Peace, Love, Appreciation & Enjoyment. 8) How to Master Your Health, Sleep, Energy & Lose Weight.*

Time will tell how this pans out. I will publish them in the order which seems most relevant and important to me and hopefully to you.

Contents

Introduction

How's your life going? We know we've been born. We know we'll die, but it's the bit in between that can, at times, be very challenging. We all have desires, but how often do we achieve them? Why doesn't life go the way we want it to? Maybe it's because we surround ourselves with other people who also have desires; except that their desires are different to ours.

But surely we all want the same thing: not to be stressed, to be happy, to have loving relationships, to enjoy our daily lives, to feel radiantly alive every day. We want to feel energised with passion and a purpose that fulfils us so much, that we wake up and leap out of bed, eager to experience the joys of the day. Is this possible?

Yes, I believe it is and I'm sure there are many people who are already living their lives in this way. But if we don't live our lives this way, at the moment, and really want to, how can we get there? The first step would be to know exactly what we want. The second step would be to take action which moves us towards this objective. The third step would be to never give up, until the objective is reached. There are two things which will increase the likelihood of us achieving our objectives, confidence and courage.

Being confident can help us in the moment, and help us stride into the future. Being courageous is exactly what is needed to overcome problems and accomplish what we want in life. Being confident and courageous will lubricate our journey through life. This book will help you master them both.

This is the second book in the "Master Your Life" series. The first one is *How to Conquer Anxiety, Worry, Fear and Stress*. Having conquered our fears the next logical step is to master our confidence and courage. Other books in this series will follow. This book is not simply a book to be read, but rather it is a practical system for change. To get the most out of it, it's helpful to understand 1) What controls your life, 2) How your beautiful mind works, and 3) How to train your beautiful mind. This is covered in the first three chapters of the book. Please note that these same chapters are also in the first book, but it is vital that each new reader who discovers this series is cognisant of this before they start the Mind Truth exercises.

CHAPTER 1

What Controls Your Life?

Your most valuable asset

What is the most valuable asset you possess? You carry it around with you at all times. It decides how stressed you are, how happy you are, who you fall in love with and marry, what type of house you live in and what car you drive. It decides how many friends you have, how fit and healthy you are, what job or career you pursue, how much money you have, how you live and how you die. It is of course your mind. How do you treat this most important treasured vessel? Do you look after it? Do you feed it well, nourish it, love it? We all know how to look after ourselves physically. We sleep, feed, exercise, wash, shower, clean our teeth. But what do we know about looking after ourselves mentally? Is our physical well-being more important than our mental well-being?

Who are you?

"Who am I?" Is a question many people ask themselves. Maybe you do too.

You are not your arms or legs or any body part, not even your mind since this is constantly changing . You are not your family or friends. You are not your health or fitness. You are not your age or weight or colour or religion or political persuasion. You are not your skills or talents or experiences or failures or successes. You are not your job or bank balance. According to Jeddah Mali, "All beauty comes out of who we are, not what we do." Who you are is more important than what you do. So, just who are you?

I find it serves me to think of myself as pure energy. If you were to ask a quantum physicist, he or she would say we are all made up of energy. Energy vibrates, and the rate of vibration changes. Ice, water and steam are all the same thing, but at different vibrations. Different human states have different vibrations too. Anxiety has a very different vibration to relaxation. Boredom has a different vibration to curiosity.

If we categorise emotions as positive or negative, some of the positive ones are: happiness, love, appreciation, enjoyment, peace, patience, fun, kindness, goodness, faith, confidence, courage, generosity, forgiveness, optimism and excitement. Some of the negative ones are: disappointment, sadness, loneliness, frustration, anger and fear. If you are pure energy, you surely want to be in a positive, pleasant state as much as possible; and when in it, try to stay in it. If you find yourself in a negative, unpleasant state you can make the effort to change it as quickly as possible. This book will help you do that. Unfortunately the predominant energy of many people is lack, struggle, fear and pain. Don't let these people influence you, whether it's the news media, print media, TV, governments, big business, associates, friends or even family. What you focus on you move towards, so focus on designing your own outstanding life. Focus and move towards what *you* want not what others want for you.

Maybe a better way of looking at who we are, is to ask a better question. Instead of asking "Who am I?" ask the question, "Who do I want to be?" and "How do I want to experience my life?" Having decided who you want to be and how you want to experience life, do everything in your power to bring it about.

The formative years

If you had been born into a very wealthy family, who loved and cherished and nurtured and encouraged you, your mind would be full of certain beliefs and truths. And if, unfortunately, you were the unloved, unwanted child of an unemployed, drug addict, single mother, who resented your presence, and constantly criticised you, then your beliefs and truths would be totally different.

When we are born, we are born with a clean slate, a clean mind, and we start filling it up from day one. In our formative years we don't have any choice as to what goes into our minds to become our truths. It's whatever is happening around us based on our environment and parental activities. The good news is that if we want to change, right now, to be predominantly in positive states such as peace, happiness, love, confidence, courage, self-esteem, appreciation and enjoyment, we can reprogram our beautiful minds.

Dr Andrew Newberg and Mark Waldman are prolific writers of over twenty books on the brain, and in their book, *How Enlightenment Changes Your Brain*, they state, "From the moment we are born, the human brain has the remarkable ability to constantly change itself. Think about who you are today and who you were a decade ago, or even last year or last month. Although you are the same person, you have learnt new skills, had new experiences, and let go of old beliefs and habits that no longer have relevance in your life." Yes, from today onwards you will continue to change. The issue is to orchestrate your *own* change, rather than random circumstances and other people's agendas changing you. This book will help you change in the direction *you* want: towards peace, happiness, love, appreciation, joy; and of course confidence and courage.

Child becomes man

"Give me a child until he is seven and I will show you the man." The origin of this quote is unclear. It could be Aristotle or the Jesuits, but whoever it is, the truth of it is clear; those early days are foundational in building the man or woman of the future.

When you were a child your mind was like a sponge to your environment, and you downloaded what was going on around you. You took in experiences, ideas, thoughts, beliefs, feelings, and you became you. But during this time you also took in worries and fears and guilt and shame and jealousies and doubts. Many of these issues from childhood are still with us, even though they don't serve us any more. They diminish and contract us as human beings. Minimising these negative traits and maximising our wonderful, positive, beautiful traits is the aim of this book and this series.

What matters now

Now that you're no longer a child, there is one thing far more important than other people's thoughts and comments, and that is your own thoughts and comments. In other words, it's the words you say to yourself and the pictures you make in your mind, which now matter and influence you and change you. When you were a young child you didn't have the freedom to choose. But now it's different. As a mature, independent thinker you do have the power to choose. You can accept or reject an idea as true or not, simply because you want to. Truths change in you constantly anyway, depending on your circumstances and experiences. Let the good stuff in. Let it change you and your truths for the better. Keep the bad stuff out. Don't let it contaminate you.

As a child you had no choice but to absorb your parents beliefs, but now you can decide for yourself and install new beliefs. As just said, beliefs change in you constantly anyway, so make sure they change to suit you. You can't focus on a positive memory or experience and a negative memory or experience at the same time, so focus on that which serves you. What you focus on expands, so focus on the positive. You can't hold two conflicting thoughts at the same time, for example, "I love travelling by car but we'll probably crash," doesn't work. You can't have sad thoughts and happy thoughts at the same time. Choose happy. You can't be confident and shy at the same time. Choose confidence. You can't be a coward and courageous at the same time. Choose courage. Since you can only think one thought at a time, if your thinking is making you stressed or sad or angry, you can substitute it with an uplifting thought. Maybe a thought of peace or happiness or appreciation, or a thought of love.

Past programming

Some of our past programming may have been debilitating with parents, teachers, friends and associates criticising us and putting us down. Some of our past programming was doubtless very good with caring parents, teachers, friends and associates who encouraged us and expected the best of us. Just one person can have a very positive, life changing impact on us, as the story below can testify.

When I went on my first ski instructor's course I could barely ski parallel. Out of the 10 classes of 20 skiers in each class, I was the third from the bottom in the bottom class. Fortunately, we had the legend who is Ali Ross as our trainer and he programmed so much confidence into me that I came to believe that I had what it takes. Even though I failed the course, I gave up my job when I got home and drove up to Scotland, where I got a job as a ski instructor. Joy of joys! "My sincere thanks go out to you, Ali. Your faith in me changed my life. You gave me confidence. You programmed me to believe in myself and my ability to teach skiing." Who has impacted you for good or bad in the past? As a child you had no option but to be programmed by others. But now it's up to you to take responsibility to decide for yourself what influences you. You can take control of your own programming.

Who is in charge of your conditioning?

According to Brian Tracy, "We are all conditioned to respond in certain ways either positively or negatively. Unfortunately most of our conditioning has occurred in a random, haphazard way, usually by accident. It's now your job to take full control over your own mental programming, to ensure that the way you automatically respond is consistent with your highest good."

Your past does not equal your future, unless you allow it. Rather, decide what you want and work towards it. This may take responsibility, self-control and courage, but it will be worth it. The effort will be temporary but the results long-lasting.

Negative emotions

What holds us back in life more than anything else? Negative emotions, especially fear! Some of the worst are fear of failure or rejection or loss or criticism. These are embedded in us as children. Since we are inexperienced, uncoordinated and self-centred at an early age, our parents are constantly correcting us. We learn we don't have the freedom to try things for ourselves, to make our own decisions, to make our own mistakes, live our own lives. We learn frustration and close ourselves down. Negative emotions abound. Unfortunately they can still be with us later in life. Overcoming them by cultivating positive traits such as happiness, love, self-esteem, appreciation, self-control, confidence and courage will make all the difference.

Our thoughts

Thoughts are things. Very important things. Our thoughts literally change our world. We must make sure our thoughts serve us well. Every thought you think has a physical reaction in your body. Every word you read fires off neurons in your brain related to that word. When we daydream, our subconscious mind takes over and sends us random thoughts and words and songs and images and conversations into our conscious mind. They come and go. This is automatic. A default setting. It takes no effort. It's easy. Understand that you and your thoughts are not the same thing. You are not your thoughts. You are the generator and observer of your thoughts.

The beauty of being a human being is that we can override debilitating or even poor thoughts by consciously choosing thoughts and words that nurture us. The most important words you will ever hear are the words you say to yourself either in your head or out loud. By changing the self-talk words, and the pictures in your head to positive, encouraging, upbuilding ones, you reduce fear, you become happier and more successful in life. The self-talk and pictures you make in your head control your feelings. Your feelings control your actions. Your actions control your results. For outstanding results use outstanding self-talk and positive pictures. Reject negative thoughts and words and pictures, and replace them with life-enhancing ones.

The default setting in our brains is designed to keep us safe and stop us from injuring or killing ourselves; and it does this by constantly looking out for threats. It is like a sentry or a look out, constantly keeping vigil. "Watch out!" "Be careful!" "Is it safe?" "Is there danger here?" It is constantly on guard. If we're not careful we can let this type of fear take over. Fortunately we can override this by acknowledging that our brain is only doing its job and by focusing on positive things we can do something about.

Many people live in a state of anxiety, worry, fear and stress. If you are to overcome these yourself and you find you are associating with negative people, it may be better to limit your association with them, so their negativity doesn't rub off on you. If you're trying to be happy and are smiling and upbeat when those around you are looking and talking miserably and enjoying a pity party, they may not appreciate your positivity. But don't let them influence you.... Don't let them bring you down to their level. Be strong, be confident, be courageous and keep smiling.

What is truth?

The truths that interest us, as we learn to master confidence and courage, are the personal truths we have internalised. Happily they're not fixed but are flexible. Many of our truths change with time. At one time many people's truth was that the world was flat. That was what they knew. It was a belief, their truth. On a more personal, individual level, if you believe you're not intelligent it will affect your whole life. If your truth is that people are basically honest and kind, you'll interact with them in a very different way to a belief that most people are dishonest and unkind. Which is true? There is no truth here, only opinion and belief. And it can be changed. If you were told as a child you were stupid, it's a rare child that thinks, "No, actually, I'm really intelligent." Now, however you can challenge any truth you want. How intelligent do you think you are now?

Intelligence

The school system when I was growing up equated a good memory to intelligence. Those who memorised the information fed to them got the top marks and the glory. While memory is important there are other intelligences too. Here are a few. Which of these apply to you?

1) Linguistic intelligence – public speakers, journalists, authors, presenters.

2) Spatial intelligence – architects, film directors, sculptors, painters, air traffic controllers.

3) Kinaesthetic intelligence – sportspeople, dancers.

4) Musical intelligence – song writers, musicians, conductors, composers.

5) Interpersonal intelligence – teachers, social workers, interactive influential people, authors, bloggers, podcasters.

6) Naturalistic intelligence – people with an affinity with nature, biologists, botanists, gardeners, animal lovers.

7) Logic/mathematical intelligence – mathematicians, scientists, detectives, programmers.

Of course, we all have different degrees of different intelligences. Some exceptional people such as Leonardo da Vinci excelled in many. The good news is that what we focus on grows, so we can decide which intelligences we want to feed and amplify. Also this means just because we may not be that intelligent in one area, such as maths or languages, doesn't mean we're not intelligent. Look for and focus on your *own* intelligences and strengths.

In their book, *Soar With Your Strengths*, Donald O. Clifton and Paula Nelson write, "Find out what you do well and do more of it; find out what you don't do well and stop doing it." Sounds like good advice to me.

My truth as a child was that I was a great football (soccer to our American friends) player, but when I was kicked off the cub scout football team at the age of 10 my truth changed. At school I was of slight build and a poor runner and not built for rugby (which the school excelled at) so my truth was that I was not sporty. But then I discovered skiing. When I started I was no better than any of my fellow recreational skiers. It was only with time, effort and practice that I became a proficient ski instructor. Since then my truth is that I'm very sporty. I now regularly workout with weights and I play squash once a week. So truths can change. The goal of this book is that regardless of the situation you are in at the present moment, you will be able to progress in the direction that you want, and achieve exactly what your heart desires.

Words change you

When it comes to your mind, to prove to yourself how the words and pictures in your brain affects your cells and the systems of your body, try this... think of sitting down and waiting for someone to serve you your favourite food dish. It arrives. It looks perfect, just how you like it. It smells wonderful. Then you take a mouthful. Your mouth explodes. It tastes out of this world... Maybe you're now salivating or feeling hungry. Or try the same with a lemon. Imagine picking up a lemon. Feel the peel. Caress it. Smell it. Rub it between your fingers. Pick up a knife and cut into it. Bits of juice spurt out. Smell the flesh of the lemon and feel the sharp odour assaulting your nostrils. Finally bite into it and chew on the flesh and peel. Once again you're probably salivating if you've played full out on this. Note that my words became a sensory experience for you. Words matter. Words cause a sensory experience or physiological responses in your mind and body.

Steer your own life.

There are three things that will completely steer the direction of your mind and life.

1) The words you say to yourself in your head. Your self-talk.

2) The images which are in your head. The pictures you make.

3) The meaning you give to the situations in your life.

I love the story of the woman who is distraught because her husband and two boys refuse to take their shoes off in the house. They walk over her pride and joy of a beautiful, new, white carpet in the lounge. Every time she sees the dirty footprints she gets upset and stressed, so goes to a psychologist for help on how to change her family's behaviour. The psychologist has her relax and see the beautiful white carpet in her mind's eye. Then he says, "Know this, that the clean white carpet represents the loneliness you feel in your heart. No one loves you. No one comes to see you. No one walks on your white carpet because you are all alone without family or friends." The situation hasn't changed, but the meaning of the situation has. Now a clean carpet means loneliness and a dirty carpet means family, friends and love. She returns home happy, to a dirty carpet. Events themselves don't affect us as much as the meaning we attached to them and the interpretation we put on them.

This can be difficult to get your head around. But it is worth the effort... There is no absolutely fixed meaning to anything in life. It is always affected by the point of view we bring to it. So what ever happens to us and whatever situation we are in, we give it meaning.

I remember getting sacked from a job I didn't want to get sacked from. I was upset, angry and stressed for a short while, until I changed the meaning and decided to look on it as an opportunity to find a better, more suitable job. I applied myself to this and a short while later, I found such a job. If we can look for and find a benefit in a situation, then although nothing has changed externally we feel better internally. We can always ask ourselves, "What good could come out of this?" Or "What meaning shall I choose that will serve me now?"

The same situation experienced by a group of people will result in a different meaning for each one. Each individual experiences the situation through the filter of their own truths. What we think is reality is only reality for the individual, so reality is personal to you. Everyone's reality is different, which can be a blessing or a curse. Don't expect anyone else to see things the way you do. Don't expect anyone else to see *you*, the way you do. They can't, but that's okay. Your job is to know yourself and be the best you, you can be, while you love them and embrace the differences.

We are all doing the best we can, given our own individual circumstances and truths. Your truths and their truths are changing all the time. Your job is to reject truths that don't serve you and absorb truths that do serve you. If you are not as happy as you want to be and your life is not everything that you dream it could be, the good news is that only one person is responsible and in control of your future. It is you, based on the truths going on in your head.

In the next chapter we'll look at the other two things that steer the direction of your mind and life; the words and pictures in your head. We'll also look at what we can do practically to make positive changes, master our minds and master our lives; and spend more time in happier, more beautiful, fun, enjoyable, confident and courageous states.

CHAPTER 2.

How Your Mind Works

"My mindset is my most critical element. My mindset is more important than my knowledge, my wealth, my everything... How you form your mindset is critically important."

Peter Diamandis

Have you ever upgraded your phone or TV or car? Very likely. We often want the latest version, expecting it to work better and give us more happiness, confidence, pride, pleasure. But how often do we upgrade the most valuable and important thing we possess, our minds? Let's not put up with an older, inferior model mind when, with a bit of time effort and fun, we can create a modern, upgraded one. You are not stuck with the mind you've got. You can make it better.

As we have seen previously, the truths that we hold in our mind are formed initially in our formative years, especially ages one to seven. However, we do keep changing and are changing constantly. Our minds are malleable and we keep changing and learning right up to the day we die. Many of our present truths and changes have happened in a haphazard way which have not necessarily served us. Now is the time to change our truths for the better, using the technique I call Mind Truths.

When you talk to yourself and encourage yourself with a positive idea or instruction, it's called an affirmation. Affirmations have been around for a long time. An early proponent of affirmations (also known as self-suggestion or auto-suggestion) was Emile Coue (26-2-1857 to 22-7-1926). He was a brilliant French health practitioner who is famous for having his patients frequently repeat, "Every day in every way I'm getting better and better." Talking of auto-suggestion, he stated, "It can wound or even kill you if you handle it imprudently and unconsciously. It can, on the contrary, save your life when you know how to employ it consciously."

A more modern proponent of affirmations was Muhammad Ali. He said, "It's the repetition of affirmations that leads to belief. And once that belief becomes a deep conviction, things begin to happen." Things certainly happened for him as he kept telling himself and the world, "I am the greatest." They can happen for you too, when you develop the skill of using Mind Truths.

So, what are Mind Truths? Mind Truths are statements that you would like to install into your mind, so that they become part of your personality, part of your way of thinking, feeling, and being; part of you. Mind Truths are statements you give to your mind. You expect your mind to process, absorb and embed what you say. There's usually a sliding scale of truth about them already. For example, if you say, "I am bold and courageous," your mind may say something like, "Okay, sometimes you are, sometimes less so." However, as you keep instructing and insisting, "I am bold and courageous," the mind will get the message and you will feel more and more bold and courageous. For this reason, I like to call these statements Mind Truths, since they become truths for your mind. They steadily grow, amplify and ripen in your mind, the more you use them.

The mind can only focus on one thing at a time, so take advantage of this and have it focus on positive Mind Truths. Try reading a book and having a conversation with someone at the same time. You can switch from one to the other, but not focus on both together. So it is with your mind. So focus on Mind Truths that encourage you, build you up, and change you. Flood your mind with Mind Truths rather than allowing indiscriminate, or debilitating thoughts to randomly pop up in your head and control you.

Since your mind does what you tell it, tell it great things. Since your mind works by repetition, keep repeating great things. Since you are a person of choice, choose to enjoy using Mind Truths. Become good at using Mind Truths. Make it a habit. Decide that Mind Truths will help you become the peaceful, happy, confident, courageous person you want to be; while you happily, confidently and courageously achieve what you want to achieve in life.

Be encouraged. Be happy. Be thrilled. Be inspired by yourself. Be a winner. Be successful. Have a great life. You are in control. Don't let your mind take in random or poor instructions from circumstances around you. Take control of your own mind. Be in charge of it. Be your own best friend. Encourage yourself and if challenges come up in the way of debilitating words or pictures override them with encouraging words and pictures. Be a loving friend and a great parent to yourself.

Parents and children

Giving correct instructions to the mind is vital for a good outcome. One of my pet peeves is when I hear parents disciplining their children with instructions such as, "Don't run," "Don't slam the door," "Don't climb up there. You'll fall off and hurt yourself." Can you see the problem? All these instructions put a negative image in the child's mind - exactly what the parent doesn't want. It's no wonder they don't respond or quickly do it again.

How much better to say, "Walk." "Close the door slowly and quietly." "When you're climbing, just be careful." This puts the right images in the child's mind so they're more likely to obey. It's exactly the same when we talk to ourselves. Giving our minds positive instructions moves us toward a positive outcome. The most important person you communicate with is yourself. You have the ability to communicate clearly with yourself through your words and pictures, so your mind will work for you, not against you. It is a skill you can develop with the help of this book.

Two wolves

As we have seen, Mind Truths are hardly a new idea and there's a lovely American Indian legend which illustrates this. Here's how the story goes...

An old Cherokee is teaching his grandson about life. "A fight is going on inside me," he said to the boy. "It is a terrible fight and it is between two wolves. One is evil. He is anger, envy, sorrow, regret, greed, arrogance, self-pity, guilt, resentment, inferiority, lies, false pride, superiority, and ego." He continued, "The other is good. He is joy, peace, love, hope, serenity, humility, kindness, benevolence, empathy, generosity, truth, compassion, and faith. The same fight is going on inside you and inside every other person too." The grandson thought about it for a minute and then asked his grandfather, "Which wolf will win?" The old Cherokee simply replied, "The one you feed."

Yes, feeding your mind with good, positive, encouraging, life-enhancing words and pictures is what Mind Truths are all about.

Your subconscious mind

If your subconscious mind is not encouraging your happiness and it throws up random or repetitive thoughts that scare you and pull you down, what can you do? You can use your conscious mind to override these thoughts and use better, more empowering words and pictures, such as you get here in these Mind Truths. Take control of your conscious mind to feed and update your subconscious mind. Give your conscious mind clear Mind Truths it can understand and work with. With time and repetition they will be absorbed and accepted by your subconscious mind. Yes, it may take a bit of time, but if you keep telling yourself something such as, "I am enough, I like myself, I love myself," your subconscious mind will start to believe it and you'll start to behave it too.

Our brains are association machines. If I say "banana" to you, you imagine a banana in your mind's eye. If I say "smile", you process that word and maybe smile yourself or imagine someone else smiling. If I say to you, "You are enough, you are kind, and you have a lovely smile," your brain must process it, and it's the same when you say it to yourself. "I am enough. I am kind and I have a lovely smile." Your brain must process it and the more you think and say it, the stronger the impact and the truer it becomes. This is how Mind Truths work.

When you tell yourself something, over and over again, it's going to embed into your mind. It's more important than someone else telling you. For example if you don't think you can do something, but someone says, "You can do it," it may be encouraging, but it doesn't mean you're likely to do it. Alternatively, if someone says, "You can't do that," but you say, "Yes, I can," and you keep telling yourself you can, that's far more effective and powerful, and will likely get results.

If you decide you're pleasing to look at, then it's true. It's your truth, your Mind Truth. If you decide you've got a good sense of humour, then it's true. It's your truth, your Mind Truth. If you decide you're kind and happy and confident and courageous, etc., etc., well, you get the idea. The Great Universal Truth is, you become what you think about and say to yourself, most of the time. Decide to master your confidence and your courage using the Mind Truths in this book.

Obsolete thoughts

We are not our thoughts and we certainly don't need to believe every thought that comes up into our head. Many of our thoughts are obsolete thoughts from the past, which are no longer valid and no longer serve us. Allow these debilitating thoughts to come and go. We can override them and move them along more quickly by focusing on thoughts that do serve us. Doing the Mind Truths in this book, will seed your mind with thoughts that serve you, until they blossom and dominate your thinking. I use Mind Truths all the time. When I catch myself thinking bad thoughts, or find myself in a bit of a mood, one simple Mind Truth I use is... "Now is the moment to smile, because now is my life." Saying this to myself interrupts myself, and gives me a clear focus for that moment. Another one I use is, "I smile and generate thoughts and feelings of peace, love, appreciation and enjoyment." I call this the Big Five, and I consciously and continually program myself to live this.

Your mind can be your best friend or your worst enemy. Befriend it. Train it so it works *for* you, not against you. Train it to be happy. Programme it with what *you* want, not what *others* want for you. The majority of our thoughts, feelings, and actions occur without any conscious awareness or involvement. It's all automated. We need to make sure what automatically comes up into the conscious mind is not debilitating, but life enhancing - thoughts of happiness, love, peace, confidence, courage, success. Reprogramming ourselves using Mind Truths will help greatly.

Your brilliant mind

To prove how brilliant your mind is and how it works, have you ever forgotten someone's name, then while you're in the shower or doing something else, suddenly the name pops into your head? Your subconscious mind was working on it all the time, while your conscious mind was not. Your subconscious mind will work on your Mind Truths even after you've stopped doing them consciously. How good is that?

While you're doing your Mind Truths, think of it like building a house. Building work starts and effort is put in, but you are not living in it yet. As time goes on and your Mind Truths build in your head, the day will come when you live in these truths. You will be living in a new mind/house that you have built yourself to your own specifications.

When we have a definite belief embedded in the mind, the mind tends to reject ideas or information that conflicts with that belief. That's why some beliefs, even silly ones, can be persistent. But you can be even more persistent and can overcome old beliefs and old Mind Truths with new ones. Yes, the more we repeat a certain thought, the more real it becomes, which is what this book is all about. Once the new ones are embedded you will have changed yourself to become the person you want to be.

Feeling the words

Thoughts and words affect our physiology and feelings. Try this. Think of a time when something really funny happened to you or think of when someone or something made you laugh out loud. Really try to get into it by seeing what you saw at the time, hearing what you heard, and remembering how good you felt. If you're playing full out, you will now be smiling and feeling good. That's what this book's all about. By soaking your mind in positive Mind Truths, you'll feel better short term; and long term you'll build up the personality traits that you want to strengthen.

The more you repeat a word, the more your brain will search inwardly for experiences or situations that match that word. Try repeating one word, such as happiness, love, smile, appreciation, confidence or courage [silently or aloud] to yourself for a couple of minutes and see what happens.

Repetition works

As Paul McKenna explains in his book, *I Can Make You Happy*, "You create habits by repetition. Each one of our thoughts and actions corresponds to a neural pathway in the brain. The more we repeat a thought or action, the stronger that pathway becomes just as a pathway across a field becomes more clear and firm the more people walk along it."

By repeating your Mind Truths, they will become embedded in your subconscious and become a permanent part of your personality. These Mind Truths will override many of the negative pathways present in your brain. They grow and become superhighways which permanently affect your subconscious mind, your conscious mind, your feelings and your actions for the better. You are upgrading your own software and it's far more important than upgrading your phone or TV or car.

Warning

When you start working on new Mind Truths, your mind may fight it. For example, you say, "I am bold and courageous," your mind may say, "Hey, what's this? This is not familiar. You're not bold and courageous. Do you remember when you were scared of a fly when you were four? When you were 10 you were scared of the bullies at school," etc, etc. But with time and repetition of Mind Truths, the mind slowly gets it. It slowly gets the message and starts to embed it.

Your mind may resist the newness of something unfamiliar. It's simply trying to protect you from an unknown something which could be a threat. The answer is to make the unfamiliar familiar. After trying a new thing a few times, it becomes familiar and the resistance goes away. It becomes familiar and safe. If you find something is hard to do, don't say it's hard, say it's unfamiliar. It makes dealing with the situation much easier. If you're not used to praising yourself, encouraging yourself, believing in yourself, start doing it and it will become familiar and a part of you. Never criticise yourself or beat yourself up, rather forgive and encourage yourself. Praise boosts self-esteem, even if it comes from you. Be your own best friend.

Many of us have brains that are wired to return to the familiar. Have you seen children watching the same film or video over and over again? We tend to shop at the same shops and buy the same food and eat the same diet. If you feel resistance when it comes to doing this new system of Mind Truths, know that it's just your brain trying to get back to what's familiar.

Equally relevant is that when doing the same thing over and over, the brain can get bored and lose momentum, so we need to recognise this and make sure we stick to the new, unfamiliar method of doing the Mind Truths until it becomes a good habit.

Even if you don't initially believe a Mind Truth, if you repeat it often enough, the belief grows and it establishes itself. Your words, pictures, and beliefs are yours to change. It's your mind. You own it. And you have the right to change it. Change your thoughts to change your feelings. Change your feelings to change your actions. Change your actions to change your results. Positive Mind Truths lead to beautiful, positive, results and successes.

The good news about your physical brain is that you can grow new neurones (brain cells) and new neural pathways. The more you do your Mind Truths, the more your brain will grow. The sooner you get these Mind Truths embedded into your subconscious, the better. The more frequently and intensely you do them, the quicker the results.

Habits

The way to create a new habit, is simply to do a new action consistently for as long a period of time as necessary. Initially, a new activity will be unfamiliar and you may forget to do it or just give up because it's easier not to do it, than do it. But with a little consistency and perseverance, the habit is formed and then it's difficult to stop and the new habit is embedded in your being. Different people pick up new habits at different rates, so don't compare yourself to anyone else. In time, it's easier to do the new habit than not do it. There's no trick to it. "Just do it," as Nike says. If you should miss, don't beat yourself up. Simply get back to it.

Repetition is the mother of skills

In order to learn any new activity or skill, it's necessary to do it again and again and again until it becomes familiar. How many times did you get on a two wheeler bike, before you could balance and go? How many times did you get in the water and splash about, before you could swim? It's the same with Mind

Truths. We need to repeat them again and again and again until they are deeply ingrained in our minds. To upgrade your mind and life takes a little time and a little effort initially, until doing your Mind Truths becomes familiar and a habit, then they're easy to do and become a normal, effortless activity. Any effort incurred to begin with will be worth it and lead to handsome dividends for the rest of your life.

You know how you sometimes get a tune that keeps popping into your mind? You hardly notice it's there. Then you're suddenly aware of it. We want the same with our Mind Truths. For example, for a while every time I walked up some steps or stairs or an escalator, I would say to myself, "Strong and Powerful!" in a rhythmic way as I went up or down. Now whenever I go up or down steps or stairs, it automatically comes into my mind. It's a neural habit and a good Mind Truth embedded.

The subconscious mind

The subconscious mind is running the show and is a repository of beliefs, habits, and actions which keep us living the way we do. If it wasn't running the show, we'd have to relearn how to walk, read, or drive a car every day. And it's powerful, as anyone who's tried to change an ingrained habit will know. But habits can be changed by creating new habits through repetition. Creating the habit of doing your Mind Truths rewards you with a master habit, which will effect other habits, as your Mind Truths catch hold and become embedded.

Strength in numbers

If you can get your friends and family involved in Mind Truths too, there are many benefits. You get social confirmation that what you're doing is valid and worthwhile. Doing anything in a group or with a partner makes it easier and more fun. Seeing others get good results is motivating for you to keep doing it. You build stronger bonds in your relationships as you progress and grow together.

Here are a few Mind Truths about Mind Truths. Read them through a few times and allow them to start preparing your mind for the wonderful journey you are about to make, as you master your confidence and master your courage.

- I accept full responsibility for mastering my own confidence and courage.

- I believe Mind Truths are a great way to master my own confidence and courage.

- I believe Mind Truths are a great way to transform myself into the person I want to be.

- I do my Mind Truths every day to create the life of my dreams.

- Every day, in every way, I'm feeling better and better and better.

- I enjoy doing my Mind Truths.

- My Mind Truths upgrade and master my mind so I feel better and better.

- I allow Mind Truths to alter my mind and life for the better.

- I enthusiastically repeat my Mind Truths often and with feeling.

- I like my Mind Truths . I love my Mind Truths .

- As I do my Mind Truths I am becoming more relaxed, happier, more confident and more courageous.

CHAPTER 3

Training Your Beautiful Mind

The measure of intelligence is the ability to change.
Albert Einstein

You cannot have a positive life and a negative mind. Joyce Meyer

The mind is everything. We are changed by our thoughts. What you think you become. Buddha

Fortune favours the prepared mind. Louis Pasteur

Yesterday I was clever, so I wanted to change the world. Today I am wise, so I am changing myself. Rumi

When you practice positive affirmations and keep your words and pictures consistent with your goals and dreams, there is nothing that can stop you being the success you are meant to be.
Brian Tracy

Your mind only responds to two things: the pictures you make in your head and the words you say to yourself. And they are very easy to change. Marisa Peer

Self-suggestion is a powerful factor in building character... it is, in fact, the sole principle through which character is built.
Napoleon Hill

If you focus on fears and doubts they become your inner reality, but when you immerse yourself in feelings and thoughts of love or peace or kindness towards others, these become your inner and outer reality. It will change your life. Mark Waldman

Self-talk means you tell yourself how to feel...how to respond. You literally say things in your mind or out loud to yourself... You have to give yourself affirmations. Brendon Burchard

Every thought matters

Your mind is magnificent. Your mind is constantly being stimulated by what goes on around you and within you. Every thought you think, every situation you experience, everything you do, changes your mind for better or worse. It's up to you to change it for better.

You become what you think about most of the time, so think good, positive, upbuilding, uplifting, energising thoughts; rather than the often present negative, life debilitating thoughts. Negative thoughts are simply memories from the past influencing the present; or anticipation of bad things to come in the future. Recognise them for what they are, just thoughts. Recognise that you are not your thoughts. Be aware that you are the recogniser and observer of your thoughts. You and your thoughts are different. Your thoughts come, they go. Let the bad ones go quickly and hold onto the good ones longer. Your mind can't hold a negative and positive thought at the same time, so overpower the negative thoughts with positive, energetic thoughts.

Your mind's Job

Your mind's primary job is to keep you safe, which it does by drawing your attention to anything that is potentially harmful or a threat. That's why bad news and misery sells, because your mind naturally pays attention to it, so you can avoid it in future. It's your hard wiring. It's your default setting. It's trying to protect you, guard you and look out for you. It's your ever present sentry and like any good look-out, it's constantly scanning for potential danger. "What's that noise?" "Careful on the road!" "Watch that person!" "Don't do that. Stay in your comfort zone." Your mind runs on fear, worry and problems. No wonder we get stressed and rundown.

Your mind doesn't care whether you're happy or not; no threat. If you're full of love and joy and peace it can't do its job. Do you know anyone who isn't "happy" unless they are whingeing and complaining about their problems? Their mind is running their show.

You don't need to believe your thoughts. You don't need to accept as true every thought you think. By being aware of your thoughts you can evaluate their validity and choose to believe them or not; to act on them or not. This puts you in control of your mind. This means you live from conscious choice and not from the default, negative programming. Manage your own mind or your mind will manage you. Tame your own mind or your mind will tame you.

You can choose your own thoughts. This is how you take control and master your thoughts and yourself. This is how your mind becomes your supporter rather than your worst enemy. So train your mind. Work with it. Instruct it. Coach it. Educate it. Your mind learns by repetition, so drill it with the Mind Truths in this book. Upgrade and master your mind with Mind Truths and watch your fears decrease and your confidence, courage and happiness increase.

Feel it

When your mind takes on a word, or picture, or thought, it also takes on the feelings associated with it. Whatever is going on in your mind triggers feelings. Because this is happening constantly and automatically we may not be so aware of it. Read these words and see if you register any feelings: death, hate, pain, kill, violence, torture. Not so nice! Shake them off and now try: peace, love, happiness, kindness, joy, appreciation, smiles. I hope you can feel the difference. You can consciously and actively avoid the thoughts, words, and pictures that are energy sapping and debilitating. Rather, consciously pour refreshing, energising and upbuilding thoughts, words and pictures into your mind until it overflows.

Recognise the difference between *move away from* states and *move towards* states. The *move away from* states are states we don't want to be in, such as fear, anger, depression and frustration. The *move towards* states are states we *do* want to be in, such as confidence, courage, peace, love, appreciation, happiness and enjoyment.

Who's running your show?

If you think your conscious mind is running your show, think again. It's your subconscious mind. If you doubt that try changing an ingrained habit by conscious force. Try dieting, or giving up smoking, or giving up sex, drugs and rock and roll. Regardless of what you want consciously, your subconscious will fight you. To combat this I find it helpful to think of bad habits as simply being familiar to my mind, whereas things I want to change are simply unfamiliar to my mind. When changing behaviour, if you think of making bad things unfamiliar and good things familiar, it takes much of the anxiety out of change. By repeating the exercises in this book, your mind gets used to doing them, they become familiar, and a good habit is formed.

What's your job?

The mind quickly and easily defaults to daydream mode. Unfortunately it often refers back to negative past programming or anxieties of things to come in the future. Your job is to train your mind. Your job is to tell your mind what you want. Tell it great things. Your mind's job is to believe what you tell it. Repetition works. Tell it great things, again and again and again. Tell it upbuilding things. It's simple, it's powerful and it works. Your mind lets in the good and bad alike, so you must choose to overpower the bad with the good. Parents know that if their children play with the "bad" kids they'll be influenced by them. Don't let your mind play with "bad" debilitating thoughts. Rather let it play with the happy, good, positive, upbuilding, thoughts that benefit you. You are free to choose, so choose thoughts that encourage and energise you. Don't think of this as discovering yourself, think of it as creating yourself. Be the creator of your mind and life, not the manager of your circumstances. Decide to encourage and build yourself up to become exactly who you want to be.

It's science

Dr Bruce Lipton is a former medical school professor and research scientist. The fly-cover of his book, *The Biology of Belief*, states, "(His research) shows that genes and DNA do not control our biology; but instead DNA is controlled by signals from outside the cell, including the energetic messages emanating from our positive and negative thoughts." So as well as reprogramming our minds for the better, we can even influence how our DNA is expressed.

When I read a book or watch a program or lecture, I take notes in a way that I feel will serve me best. I'd like to include here the exact notes I took on watching one of Dr Lipton's lectures... "My mind controls my genes. My mind controls my life. I can change my mind and my life and biology. Also the environment controls the genes and biology and life. What I think controls my health. My body is just a reflection of what's going on in my mind. Change beliefs and attitudes about life I change my biology. Placebo/nocebo. Heal/kill. Don't be a victim of your belief system. Most of my thoughts are negative and abundant. Be aware and change the thoughts to positive ones. Life changer."

In conclusion, be aware of the thoughts going on in your mind. With awareness comes power. The power to choose. Your deciding to dismiss debilitating thoughts, while hanging onto positive thoughts, will change you for the better. You can program your mind with Mind Truths and become familiar with upbuilding, energising, thoughts and take your life to a higher level.

Read the Mind Truths below. Do it with feeling in an emotionally charged way for maximum benefit. Chapter 5 will give you suggestions as to different ways to use your Mind Truths.

Your Beautiful Mind Mind Truths

- My mind is the most valuable thing I have.

- My mind is the most beautiful and powerful thing in the universe.

- I am learning to control my mind.

- My mindset is my most important and valued asset.

- My mindset is changing anyway, so I make sure it changes in the direction I want.

- I am not my thoughts, but I am the observer of my thoughts.

- My greatest power is to choose my own thoughts.

- I look after my mind. I protect it from harmful input and I feed it positive input.

- I allow my bad mind habits to become unfamiliar to me, while I make new mind habits familiar.

- I let bad thoughts evaporate, but I hold on to good thoughts.

- I decide what to put in my mind and what not to put in my mind.

- My most important skill is being able to communicate with myself by programming my mind.

- I tell my mind what I want. I tell it great things.

- I appreciate that my mind is just trying to keep me safe, but I want to live in a happy, peaceful, loving, appreciative, confident, courageous, energised place.

- I train my mind or it will train me.

- I give clear direct instructions as to how I want my mind to operate.

- I become what I think about, so I think good, happy, encouraging, upbuilding, confident, courageous, thoughts.

- My mind learns by repetition so I repeat my positive Mind Truths often.

- My Mind Truths change me. They change me internally in my mind and emotions, and externally in my actions.

- I absorb my Mind Truths like a sponge and allow them to positively influence me.

- I enjoy doing my Mind Truths.

CHAPTER 4

Confidence

Where you are today is really a function of your current confidence level. Dan Sullivan

Confidence is nothing more than a series of neural patterns that have been reinforced. John Asaraf

You can develop the kind of irrepressible self-confidence you desire by simply repeating certain thoughts and actions over and over until they are driven deep into your subconscious mind and take on a power of their own. Brian Tracy

The most beautiful thing you can wear is confidence. Blake Lively

Confidence comes from discipline and training. Robert Kiyosaki

Self-confidence is the foundation of all great success and achievement. Brian Tracy

When you have confidence you can have a lot of fun. And when you have fun, you can do amazing things. Joe Namath

Just be confident. I think confidence is the most attractive part of a person. Curtis Jackson

With confidence, you have won before you have started. Marcus Garvey

We all need confidence

We all need as much confidence as we can muster. Life is unpredictable, challenging, and scary at times. The more confidence we have the easier life becomes and the better we feel. Confidence helps oil our way through life. Having confidence means your whole life is likely to be more pleasant and successful. While being bold and courageous are very necessary for a progressive life, they don't feel particularly good. Confidence on the other hand feels good. It is well worth upgrading, amplifying and mastering.

What is confidence?

Confidence can be described as having a belief or certainty that you are able to handle a particular situation. The origin of the word confidence comes from the Latin confidere, "to have full trust or reliance." So having confidence in oneself means being able to trust and rely on oneself, regardless of what's happening around us. I like the definition that Dr Joan Rosenberg has for it. "The deep sense that we can handle the emotional outcome of whatever we face or whatever we pursue." Confidence can be situational. You may be confident in one area of life in which you are more familiar, since you have gained certain experience and skills. You may have little or no confidence when starting a new activity, but that will soon change as knowledge and experience brings you familiarity. Having general self-confidence will allow you to take on new things with the belief that you can progress in that area. Self-confidence is a feeling that you can handle what life throws at you.

How important is confidence?

It's so important that it's worth billions of dollars on a global scale. A lack of confidence in the factors governing the stock market can wipe billions off the value of companies. On a personal scale you can probably think of people you have confidence in and you're probably drawn to them. You probably avoid people you have no confidence in. Your job is to be the person others have confidence in. Build your confidence using the techniques in this chapter and the Mind Truths in chapter 6, and watch your life get better and better.

Confidence is an energiser. The more confidence you have the better you do. Being confident doesn't mean you compare yourself to others and look down on them. That's arrogance. Do you know anyone who is arrogant? They have low self-esteem and want to elevate themselves by diminishing others. That's not you.

Does your confidence come from outside of yourself, i.e. from other people, or do you generate your own confidence? By all means be encouraged by other people but, don't be dependent on anyone else for your own confidence. Don't allow other people to adversely affect you or influence you. Take full responsibility for your own confidence. It is an ability that you can amplify and expand for yourself.

One for the men

According to relationship blogger Marnie Kinross, "Women are attracted to men with confidence because we feel that these men will be able to take care of us no matter what happens. Simply put, confident men do. And they do it well. Being around a man who knows what to do is intoxicating." What man doesn't want his woman to be intoxicated and have confidence in him. So men, this is definitely something worth working on.

One for the women

According to Nicole Scherzinger, "Girl power is about loving yourself and having confidence and strength from within." Idelette McVicker says, "There are few things more beautiful on a person than confidence. Women who wear it radiate strength, passion and conviction... When a woman knows who she is, why she is, and what she's supposed to do (she is) absolutely gorgeous." Oscar de la Renta feels the same way since he said, "The qualities I most admire in women are confidence and kindness." I think many men would agree with that.

Taking on new challenges

It would be wonderful if we could be instantly confident when we start something new or set a new goal. Unfortunately this probably isn't the case. So how can you get confident at something? You have to pay the price. First of all you need to decide to commit and be clear about exactly what you want to achieve.

You decide to go for it regardless of what it takes to get there. At his stage you may not even know *how* to get there. Next, you need to muster up the courage and take action. Taking action will lead to skills and competence, which will lead to confidence and results. Throughout this process there are things we can do to oil the wheels of confidence. Doing your Mind Truths is great for general self-confidence, or before doing anything where confidence would help. The following techniques can be used when particular events need even more confidence.

- **Detach Yourself**... One trick to confidence, is being detached from the outcome. If you can do this (detach from the outcome), it's no longer a do or die situation, or a matter of life and death. If the boy walking across the dance floor to ask the girl to dance, accepts that he may or may not get a dance and that's okay, then his self-esteem and confidence are still in one piece. He can focus on the courage needed to walk across the dance floor and ask the girl. Accepting the possibility of failure, as well as the prospect of success takes the pressure off and keeps the confidence intact. Also, just because you failed doesn't mean you are a failure. Failure is often necessary for progress, so instead, be happy that you tried. Try again, but this time with the wisdom you learnt from the failure. Failure and confidence are separate. Don't connect any failure you have to your confidence. Don't allow any failure to dent your confidence.

- **Remember**... Chill out, relax and take a few deep breaths. Now remember a time in the past when you felt confident. See what you saw, hear what you heard, feel how you felt. Really get into this. Allow your whole being to take on the confidence you felt on that occasion. Now keep bathed in that confidence and imagine a forthcoming situation that will require your confidence. Take that confidence into the new situation and see things going perfectly. Hear what do you want to hear. Feel the confidence surging through your body, radiating out for all to see. Do this several times and feel your confidence grow more and more each time.

- **Posture**... The mind and body are intimately linked so thinking confident thoughts will activate a more confident posture. Equally, taking up a confident posture will activate a more confident mind. So one way to become more confident is to take up a confident posture and think positive and confident thoughts. Never talk down to yourself. If you catch yourself thinking debilitating thoughts such as, "Oh no," "I can't," "This is bad," then stop, readjust your posture and say the opposite, "Oh yes", "I can do this," "This is good." If you keep on doing this you will reset your muscle memory as regards posture. Also you instruct your mind so that instead of automatically thinking discouraging thoughts, you are generating upbuilding encouraging thoughts. A new confident you will become your default setting.

- **Visualisation and Imagination**... Visualisation and imagination have powerful effects on our confidence. When you look forward to an event that needs your confidence, the first thing to do is spend a few moments imagining what can go wrong. Yes – what can go wrong; because fear of the unknown knocks our confidence. So, anticipate what could go wrong and then, most importantly, imagine how you will deal with it should it occur. Always see yourself handling the issue in an empowering way. The next thing to do is imagine a perfect event. Imagine everything going exactly the way you want it to. The next thing to do is imagine the situation *after* the event. It's all gone well and you are now completely relaxed and looking back with pleasure. You are creating a memory of the event. Psychologically if you have a memory of the event and it went well, doing it again will be easier and more familiar. Do this several times and watch your confidence grow each time.

- **The Perfect You**... Stand up and imagine the perfect, confident you is standing straight in front of you, facing you. Perfect you is about a couple of metres away from you. Study the perfect you. Note the posture, imagine how he/she feels, what's the expression on the face, how does he/she project into the world. The perfect you now turns around. Step forward and into the perfect you. As you do take on the posture, the feelings and project this confidence into the world. Really work it, feel it, become it, remember it. Then step back out of your perfect self but keep the confidence you've just experienced. Do this several times and watch your confidence grow each time. You can also use this technique to amplify other qualities such as happiness, courage, appreciation, love and self-esteem.

- **Beg, Steal or Borrow**... Beg, steal or borrow someone else's confidence. Similar to the last exercise, you can do this with someone you admire, someone who has supreme confidence in the area you want confidence in. Imagine them performing in the situation that you are preparing for. They are brilliant, full of confidence and performing perfectly. Go behind them and see the scene as they see it. Now imagine stepping into their body. It may help to do it in slow motion. Allow your body to synchronise with theirs. Take up their posture, look through their eyes, hear what they hear, say what they say and feel how they feel; totally and completely confident. Stay with them as they perform and as you merge with them in experiencing their confidence. Now step forward out of them but keep every ounce of confidence with you. They disappear, so you are now performing alone and it is going perfectly. Add your own authenticity and personality to the situation and enjoy! Do this several times and feel your confidence build each time. You thereby activate the first of the two steps to skilful achievement; that of copying or modelling someone who already knows how to do it. The second step is to repeatedly practice the new skill for yourself (mentally and physically) until it becomes a habit.

Power poses

There are certain movements or poses which are associated with confidence, courage or power or determination or motivation or recognition of a job well done. Here are four that you can do to increase your confidence.

1) The Acknowledgement Pose.

Pavarotti was a man confident in his singing ability and ability to entertain his audience. When he finished singing he would often stand in front of a cheering, adoring audience with his eyes closed, his face turned up and his arms outstretched. His face said it all. He was bathing in their appreciation and in the knowledge that he done a great job and the audience had loved it. Imagine a future event that requires your confidence. Stand as Pavarotti did. Take up the acknowledgement pose yourself. Imagine it went perfectly. The people are responding to you as enthusiastically as the Pavarotti crowd. You can amplify the experience by saying things like, "Thank you," "Very kind," "I appreciate that." Really feel their appreciation, their love for you, their acknowledgement of a job well done.

2) The Superman Pose.

Imagine superman standing there, solid, head up with his feet apart and hands on hips. He's ready, he is confident, he will get the job done. Take up the superman pose yourself. You can also say things like, "I'm ready," "I'm confident," "I can do this." Here are a few more:- I am special. I am authentic. I am world-class. I am awesome. I am fantastic. I am remarkable. I am spectacular. I am formidable. I am magnificent. I am outstanding. I am brilliant. I am eloquent. I am splendid. I am radiant. I am sparkling. I am impressive. I am phenomenal.

3) The Squinch.

A bit like the proverbial *deer in the headlights* we may see scared people open their eyes wide and lean their head back. The squinch is the complete opposite of this. With a confident smile on your face, squint the eyes up slightly and tilt the head forward and gently nod. You can also talk to yourself and say things like, "I can do this." "I am good at this." "I am confident."

4) Make Your Move.

You may have seen the New Zealand rugby team perform the "Haka" before a match. It's a series of power moves with chants. When English footballers score a goal you can often see them perform a power move in celebration of their goal. They may stand firm, feet solidly apart. They often clench their fists punching the air or bringing their arm up and down while pulling a face and shouting, "Yes, Yes." You can copy this move or make up your own move; one that feels empowering to you. The thing here is to "make your move" while preparing for a situation where confidence is needed.

CHAPTER 5

How to Use Your Mind Truths

P lease don't think that reading through this book once will transform your life. It will take a little time and a little effort. But it will be worth it. You are constantly changing anyway. You may as well change in the direction you choose; set your own sails, be your own captain. Instruct your beautiful mind to take you to new, exciting places. According to Ben Hardy PhD, "You...need daily practices to trigger the identity of who you intend to be." Mind Truths must be repeated often and with emotional feeling while you are confident that they are going into and changing your mind. At Romans 12:2 the Bible says, "Stop being moulded by this system of things, but be transformed by making your mind over…" Don't let other people and their ideas (this system) mould you. Transform and mould yourself. Build yourself up. Be actively reinventing yourself for the better.

Be aware that your mind may play tricks on you, if it wants you to stay the same; but you must be ruthless. Take control. Do what needs to be done to get the results you want. Prime your mind. Overwhelm your mind with positive Mind Truths, in the area you want to improve in. Practice, practice, practice. Repeat,

repeat, repeat. Make doing your Mind Truths a habit. Repeat your Mind Truths until they become a habit. The more power, feeling and energy you put into them, the quicker and easier they will grow.

Below are different ways you can do your Mind Truths. Make it as easy as you can. Do which ever of them that you think will be most doable and most fun.

Don't be overwhelmed if you feel there are too many Minds Truths. Simply choose a number that you can cope easily with and work with these. I sometimes work with one or two cards worth. It works well for me. It makes it easy and very doable.

If you are feeling apprehensive just before you do these Mind Truths, you will find that as you do them your mind has to focus on what it's doing and it shuts down any negative thoughts you may have. This works even better when you say them aloud. This works even better if you do them with someone else since part of your focus will be on them.

1) Read the Mind Truths from the book silently, but with energy and feeling.

2) Read the Mind Truths from the book with emotion, but hearing the words in your head. ie, speaking them silently to yourself.

3) Read the Mind Truths aloud with feeling.

4) Read the Mind Truths aloud with feeling while pacing the room, with attitude. Or while you're outside enjoying nature.

5) Copy or print out the relevant Mind Truths on paper, so you readily have them to hand. It's easy to pick up a sheet of paper and read.

6) Write your Mind Truths on 3 x 5 cards and keep them together with a rubber band. Your writing hand is connected directly to your brain. According to Dan Sullivan, 40% of the brain is connected to that hand. So this is a very valid and effective strategy for your transformation. Write in the colour ink you think will imprint on your mind most firmly. Write in your best, neatest handwriting. This sends a powerful message to your mind that you're serious about this, that this is important. When I use words such as great, fantastic, wonderful, if you can think of a better word which resonates more strongly with you, use your word not mine. Read your Mind Truths frequently. Energise your day by doing them first thing in the morning. Even before you get out of bed, perhaps. Do them in bed last thing at night before going to sleep. Do them many times during the day. Use 'dead' time such as while commuting, between activities, on public transport or as a passenger in a car. Involve the driver. Do them while waiting around. You could time how long it takes to do them once, so you know the time commitment for each reading. You could set a timer to go off every hour or two or three to remind yourself to do them. If you feel there are too

many Mind Truths to cope with try this. Write them all out on 3 x 5 cards anyway, then decide how long to read them for, say two or five minutes. Set a timer and do your cards for two to five minutes, then stop regardless of how many you've read. Next time just continue from where you left off. This way you will cycle through your Mind Truths nice and easily. Alternatively you could pick out your top 10 or top 20 Mind Truths, write them on your cards and work with them. Keep your cards on your person so they are easily accessible when you have a free moment to do them in.

7) Record the Mind Truths you're working on, (on your phone maybe) then play them back to yourself frequently. When I wake up, I often play the Mind Truths I am working on that day, before I even get out of bed.

8) Use your phone alarm or get a repeat timer app, setting it to go off at various times during the day. When it goes off do your Mind Truths.

9) Find a friend or family member to do the Mind Truths aloud with you.

A) One person reads one line and the other person reads the next line.

B) One person reads one line then the other person reads the same line.

C) One person reads one line then the other person repeats the line without reading it. Swap

D) One person reads one line and the other person says it back to them in the second person. eg, First person "I am enough. I like myself. I love myself." Second person, "You are enough. You like yourself. You love yourself." Swap.

10) See if you can memorise some of your Mind Truths, then you can say them silently or aloud to yourself any time you want.

11) Teachers: Do the Mind Truths with your pupils. Create classes around Mind Truths

12) Parents: Do appropriate Mind Truths with your children. It's good bonding and great for their development.

A) Read appropriate Mind Truths to young children at bedtime.

B) Use them as a teaching aid to help them learn to read.

C) Record the Mind Truths you want to install in them with your voice and using their name in the 2nd person. They are sure to play it often.

D) If children need practice in writing, have them write out relevant Mind Truths. What could be better for them? If you yourself use cards they may want to have their own cards.

Be aware of how you feel before you start your Mind Truths. Notice how you feel after doing them. You'll likely be feeling much better and more confident in your chosen area.

CHAPTER 6

Confidence Mind Truths

- I am confident. I am a confident person. Confidence is a big part of my personality.

- I accept the responsibility of mastering my own confidence.

- I see myself as an extremely confident person.

- I see myself as the confident person I want to be.

- I feel good about myself.

- I am safe. I am whole. I am in control.

- I am valuable and important.

- I am completely comfortable in my own skin. I am happily authentic.

- I am enough. I like myself. I love myself.

- I am a good person. I'm trustworthy. I trust myself and other people trust me too.

- I am unique and happy to be so.

- I am bold and courageous.

- Whatever is happening in my life I can confidently deal with it.

- I trust myself and can always rely on myself.

- I have the confidence to follow my heart. I make small decisions with my head, but big decisions with my heart.

- I increase my confidence by thinking about my good points. (Stop and think)

- I do more, share more, give more, create more, grow more, progress more.

- I confidently cope well with my life.

- As I go about my day, I have the posture of a confident person. I sit, stand and walk confidently. I talk confidently too.

- It doesn't matter where I've come from or what happened in the past. I am confidently moving towards a great future.

- I am intelligent and use my time, energy and resources to deal effectively with any situation. I am confident in my ability to handle any issue.

- I can do what I set my mind to do. I am confident and determined.

- I accept my current situation, but confidently take action to improve it and progress.

- I decide on which goals to pursue and which to abandon.

- Once my goal is set I focus my attention on the activity the goal requires and then enjoy the journey.

- I don't focus on what I *don't* want, I focus on what I *do* want.

- I decide what I want and I confidently go for it.

- I create big goals for myself, but break them into small manageable steps; then I take action.

- I confidently take action even when I'm uncertain or don't feel ready.

- I confidently take action until I reach my goals.

- I confidently take risks. I make mistakes and learn from them.

- When I fail, I learn from my failure and move on more intelligently.

- I fail forward and confidently bounce back up.

- I course correct as necessary to ensure I reach my goal.

- I refuse to take 'no' for an answer. I take 'yes' for an answer.

- I take on new things with confidence.

- I take control of myself and my life and I confidently make things happen.

- I am persistent and completely unstoppable.

- I don't do mediocrity. I do mastery.

- I am worthy and smart enough to achieve my goals.

- I make a positive difference in other peoples lives.

- People like me because I'm interested in them and I make them feel important.

- I am equal to everyone else and no worse or better.

- I am not a victim. I am a victor.

- I am bullet-proof against rejection.

- I do not need to impress anyone.

- I am not thrown by the criticism of others or blown up by their praise.

- I don't need other people's approval. I approve of myself.

- I gratefully accept compliments, but I don't need them.

- I don't compare myself to others. I am unique. I'm different and glad of it.

- I am confident enough to forgive everyone, to appreciate everyone, to love everyone and to enjoy everyone.

- I remember when I was confident in the past. (Stop and remember.)

- I am confident now and will be in the future.

- I believe in myself and my ability to live confidently.

- I confidently express who I am.

- I live my life with passion and purpose.

- I accept rejection and failure as part of life.

- I confidently take risks. I make mistakes, sometimes fail, but always learn.

- When I need confidence to do something, I do it without being attached to the outcome.

- I confidently handle what life throws at me.

- I am confident and courageous enough to rise above moments of stress, knowing I can meet any challenge.

- I am a force of confidence and positive energy.

- I trust and follow my instincts.

- I have a wonderful mind that works well and I'm using it to become more confident.

- I choose to be unbounded, where anything is possible.

- I confidently take the action needed to live the life of my choice.

- I am at peace with myself and the world around me.

- Having confidence is a familiar feeling for me.

- Every day in every way I'm getting more confident.

- I am unshakeable in my confidence.

- I am confident. I am a confident person.

CHAPTER 7

Courage

You will never do anything in this world without courage. It is the greatest quality of the mind, next to honour. Aristotle

Life shrinks or expands in proportion to one's courage. Anies Nin

Courage is the power to let go of the familiar. Raymond Lindguist

What we fear doing most, is usually what we most need to do. Tim Ferriss

He who is not courageous enough to take risks, will accomplish nothing in life. Muhammad Ali

Courage is the doorway to change. Ben Hardy

When the going gets tough, the tough get going. Joseph Kennedy

We will do more for others than for ourselves. And in doing something for others, we find a reason for courage and our cause for focus and excellence. Brendan Burchard

Courage, above all things, is the first quality of a warrior. Carl von Clausewitz.

Courage is resistance to fear, mastery of fear, not absence of fear. Mark Twain

Success takes courage

What do the following people have in common? Mahatma Gandhi, Neal Armstrong, Rosa Parks, Nelson Mandela, Steve Jobs, Oskar Schindler, Charles Lindbergh, and Edmund Hillary? They are all known to us for their courageous acts, whether physical or mental or both.

What about Rocky, Luke Skywalker, Bilbo Baggins, Robin Hood, Ben Hur, James Bond, and Harry Potter? They may be fictional characters, but they are also known to us because we value people who overcome their challenges with courage. You may not have to change the world or save the world, but by being courageous you can change *your* world and the people in it. Courage is required when an action is above or outside of your comfort zone.

What is courage?

Of course, courage is not the absence of fear, but the ability to take action despite fear. It's the mental or moral strength to act, persevere and withstand risk, difficulty, fear or danger. It's taking action in the face of uncertainty or threats. Courage is deciding to act and then following through.

Courage means facing your challenges. Courage means overcoming personal limitations in pursuit of a full life. Courage means feeling the fear and doing it anyway. Courage means pursuing a passion or goal even if it's hard to do. Courage means being authentic in deciding who you are and then living it. Courage is accepting responsibility for all your actions. Courage is pursuing you own course of action, regardless of the influences of others.

Since we are all different, what scares one person could be a walk in the park for another. However we all will be tested as we travel along the pathway of life. Often the huge benefits of acting despite fear are monumental and long-lasting, compared to the relatively short period when courage is necessary.

When I wanted to change the direction of my life from being a ski instructor to a teacher of English as a foreign language I took a teaching course. The first time I had to go in front of a class and actually teach, I was absolutely terrified. I've never been so scared in all my life. After a quick trip to the toilet (narrowly avoiding disaster pants) I took courage and faced the lions in their den. It turns out they were pussycats, and very nice ones too. It's good to remember that much of the fear we feel is simply in our heads. Anyway, having passed the course I was able to get a job teaching English in Aosta in the Italian Alps; surrounded by some of the best Italian ski resorts. I could ski for pleasure but teach for a living. A great result and huge benefit for overcoming my fears of learning new teaching skills and going into the classroom. Can you remember doing something that scared you, but in hindsight gave you a great result? What are you facing at the moment, where facing fear and taking action could change your life for the better?

One thing about doing something new and fearful is that the more you do it, the more familiar it becomes, and the more confident you get. Fear diminishes as familiarity increases. The more I went into the classroom and the more familiar it became to me the more I relaxed. Then I started to enjoy it. A few years later I wrote a textbook and opened my own school using the textbook as the course material. You never know what the future holds when you overcome your fears and take action with courage.

In his book *High Performance Habits,* Brendan Burchard puts it this way, "The kinds of courageous acts that you are proud of at the end of your life are those where you faced uncertainty and real risk, where the stakes mattered, when you did something for a cause or person beyond yourself, without any assurance of safety, reward or success." He goes on to say, "Courage is the cornerstone habit of high performance." Being courageous means stepping outside of your comfort zone when you don't feel like it. But as we have seen, the aftermath of courage can be life changing. It can take you to places you could only dream of.

Unfortunately courage and boldness require effort and feel uncomfortable so we tend to avoid doing things that require them. Unfortunately by avoiding them we are likely to stay exactly where we are, and we inhibit progress to greater things. Any breakthrough you want in your life requires, first commitment to the undertaking, then the courage to do what needs to be done, even if it's way outside your comfort zone. As you start to get results the balance between courage and confidence changes. You need less courage but the confidence starts to grow. Confidence tempered with humility equals power. That's what we want; to acknowledge and feel our own power.

Courage is influential

When others observe you engaging in courageous acts it influences them. Whether you're a parent, teacher, colleague, or friend, your boldness can be "encouraging" and have a positive effect on them.

Courageously giving to others

We will very often do more for others then we will for ourselves. The process of setting up and starting my own English language school was very challenging. But what fuelled the courage needed to do it was the thought of how the pupils would enjoy their lessons while learning to speak, read and write English. By focusing on *them* I was able to overcome my fears. I really wanted to contribute to their successes. What do you care enough about, that could cause you to take courageous action, to help or resolve a situation? Who do you care enough about helping, that would require you to courageously stand up and take action?

Several courages

Courage is only one word, but there are different types of courage. The courage of facing a terminal disease is different to the courage of participating in a challenging sport, which is different to quitting a safe job you hate, to face the uncertainty of a different job. Here are some different types of courage.

- Have the courage to live your own life in your own way, even if others don't understand it. This could mean going against the wishes of family or friends. This means not picking up bad habits, just because your friends are doing it. It means you believe in your own convictions and are prepared to standby them regardless of the opposition. It means not conforming to the expectations of others and being willing to authentically show your true self, even if it means risking social disapproval or criticism. It means having your own opinions and expressing them even if it differs from others. This courage means getting out of your comfort zone. As Steve Jobs said, "Have the courage to follow your heart and intuition, everything else is secondary." By overcoming fearful tendencies with courage we are more likely to take the necessary action to live the life of our own choosing. Only you can decide what living courageously means. Also by focusing and taking courageous actions, life becomes refreshingly simpler. Distractions become less important and fade away leaving a feeling of direction and control.

- Feats which require physical courage, while often entered into willingly still take courage. This could mean the risk of pain, injury or even death. Firefighters running into a burning building; soldiers facing people trying to kill them; climbing the highest mountains in the world; canoeing the dangerous rapids; record-breaking in sports; contact sports such as rugby or boxing; skydiving; horse racing. When the risks are high and involve pushing the physical limits of your body, this takes courage. For us mere mortals it may be as simple as starting a new challenging sport or activity that is new to us.

- Have the courage to face suffering and not let it take you down. Wallowing in self-pity could be an easy tendency when compare to the courage needed to fight and overcome suffering. Whether it's losing a loved one, battling a terminal disease, becoming disabled, battling against life's challenges, or simply feeling isolated and lonely, when suffering occurs it's time to dig deep, overcome and move on. This takes courage.

- Have the courage to stand up for what is right. Standing up to the bully at school or work; refusing to lie, cheat or steal when those around you are doing it; standing up to oppressive political regimes. When you decide what's right and stick to it despite pressures or opposition, this takes courage. This is moral courage.

- Have the courage to let go of the familiar and seek new horizons. Moving to a new area, changing job, joining a club, taking up a new hobby or sport, starting a business, letting go of false friends who don't support you, all these things mean facing uncertainty. You can't be courageous and comfortable at the same time. When necessary choose uncertainty but with courage. You will never feel one hundred percent ready to set foot into the unknown, so you will need to take courageous action when you're not completely ready for it.

- Have the courage to go for your goals. Courage can be looked on as a skill. The more you use your courage muscle the stronger and more skilfully confident you will become. Who do you admire, the wimp who plays safe and always lives in his or her comfort zone or the one who knows what he wants and goes for it despite the risks and difficulties? You decide to be that person and use the Mind Truths below to help move your life in the direction you want. Ray Edwards is a successful blogger and copywriter, but it wasn't always this way. He tells of how in his younger days he felt the fear of pain. He says, "I... was also influenced by a fear of pain, the pain of poverty, the pain of a meaningless existence. The pain of a lacklustre life I did not enjoy. The pain of not feeling a connection or contribution in the world. The pain of feeling like I did not have what it took to succeed." Fear of failure and fear of not being enough, are real fears for many. If you come from a family or environment where failure is the norm and success is, "those people, not us," it can be very difficult to rise above this kind of conditioning. But to overcome this fear, know what you want and go for your goals, to live the life of your choice. Courageously take the necessary action until the goal is reached. If this applies to you, I'm sure this book will be incredibly helpful in accelerating your splendid journey through life.

Power poses.

See the four power poses in chapter 4 (confidence). Try doing these poses. As well as confidence builders they can be used as courage builders.

Fear or excitement

Imagine a group of girls and boys on a rollercoaster. They're screaming like mad as the carriage races around the track. Are they scared or excited? Do they feel fearful or thrilled? Or imagine the boy who plucks up the courage to walk across the empty dance floor to ask the beautiful girl for a dance. Is it fear of failure and embarrassment or the exciting prospect of a potential encounter? Or what about getting on a plane. Is it fear of flying or excitement of the holiday to come?

Fear and excitement are very similar feelings in our bodies. We can use this to our advantage. When we feel fear, instead of simply going with it, and accepting it, we can tell ourselves that we are excited. Repeating the simple Mind Truth, "This is exciting. I am excited," can reduce or eliminate the unpleasant fear and turn it into a feeling of pleasant anticipation or excitement.

I must tell you that while I've been preparing this chapter all my focus has been on courage. Despite the apprehension that maybe people won't be interested in this book, I felt my courage expand and grow during the preparation and writing of it. Work this chapter yourself, especially the Mind Truths, and feel *your* courage expand and grow too.

CHAPTER 8

Courage Mind Truths

- I am courageous. I am a courageous person. Courage plays a big part in my life.

- I face life courageously. I face my challenges with courage.

- I am bold. I take bold steps. I take bold action.

- Fortune favours the bold.

- I think big and I play big.

- I am unshakable in my courage.

- When I need to let go of the familiar and face uncertainty, I do so with courage.

- I have the courage to deal with the unknowns of life.

- I regard my problems as challenges.

- I don't shrink back, but courageously face any difficulties or obstacles.

- I courageously expand my comfort zone.

- I courageously take action, despite feeling fear. I feel the fear and do it anyway.

- I am courageously willing to try something that might not work.

- I don't avoid life's challenges. I respond quickly to them.

- I don't put off things I should do. I take prompt action.

- I reflect on what's on the other side of my challenges.

- I courageously pursue my goals and passions despite the risks.

- I often act outside of my comfort zone.

- I decide at what level I want to play the game of life.

- I live a bold life and take chances and risks.

- I love trying to master new challenges.

- I spread my wings, jump courageously and fly.

- I don't do fear, I do excitement.

- I honour the struggle of my progress.

- Suffering is no big deal. I happily suffer now to reap the rewards later. Facing fear now equals rewards later.

- I overcome suffering by digging deep, taking courage and moving on.

- I see struggle as a necessary, important and positive part of my journey through life.

- I value authenticity. I am authentic in my dealings with myself and others.

- I never let anyone else define who I am.

- I walk my own path regardless of the direction others walk.

- I do the right thing, even if it means being judged or criticised.

- I find someone and something to fight for. I enjoy the service of others. I have the courage to serve others.

- I act courageously despite any indifference or opposition from others.

- I am an example of courage to others.

- I do not achieve my successes by accident. I courageously take risks that lead to my desired results.

- Even when it's difficult, I speak up for myself.

- I have the courage to fight for what I believe in.

- If something scares me, there is magic on the other side.

- I face my fears and do it anyway.

- I remember when I was courageous in the past.

- I am courageous now and will be in the future.

- I courageously take responsibility for my life.

- I courageously take responsibility for any actions I take.

- I courageously overcome my personal limitations in pursuit of the life of my choosing.

- I have the courage to be myself.

- I have the courage to express who I really am.

- I live my life own life in my own way.

- I am capable of remarkable things that I could never foretell and would never experience without taking courageous action.

- I do not allow fear to stop me living the life I desire. I act courageously.

- I don't wait for the good things to happen in my life. I go out and make them happen.

- I focus on what I want and I go for it.

- I have the courage to fight for what I love. I have the courage to follow my heart.

- I know what's worth fighting for. My life's worth fighting for.

- I am bold. I bold steps. I take bold action.

- I am courageous. I am a courageous person.

CHAPTER 9

Helping Yourself and Helping Others

You never know how far reaching something you say, think or do today, may impact the lives of millions tomorrow.
BJ Palmer

Are you pleased with the contents of this book? Do you feel it has given you good value? Have you learnt something new? Are you changing? Has your time with the book, been time well spent? I certainly hope so, and I'd like to think I have succeeded in helping you become closer to the person you want to be. I hope you enjoy using this book, as much as I enjoyed writing it. And I hope you continue to work with your various Mind Truths, as I still do.

I must congratulate you for finishing this book, however it's not really the finish, but rather a new beginning. As we know change can be difficult. Wanting to change, but not knowing how, is most frustrating. You are now in the know. You have in your hands a very simple but fun, workable system for upgrading and mastering your confidence and courage and life. Use it, work it, keep at it, and your life will be changed for ever. And so will the lives of those you touch.

If you would like to get in touch with me I'd be delighted to hear how this book with its Mind Truths have affected your life. You can contact me through my website paulbooth.org.

After you have mastered confidence and courage, what's next? Consider getting the next book in this series so you can master your self-esteem, your self-control and your responsibility.

Giving of yourself and contributing to the well-being of others is a fine thing to do. It brings much happiness to the giver as well as the receiver. It's a win win. It is my passion and purpose to spread more peace, love, appreciation, enjoyment and well-being through my books and public speaking. I invite you to help me do this. In doing so you spread more happiness and well-being in *your own* world. You could do six things...

1) Do you know anyone who is stressed or needs more confidence and courage? You could buy a copy of this book for them. They are sure to appreciate it.

2) Help others by involving them in the exercises in this book. It will of course help you too.

3) Recommend this book to your friends and social network.

4) Do you have any contacts with any schools, colleges, universities, educational establishments, charities, associations, clubs, companies, organisations, events, conventions, etc? Please send me their details. Or suggest they

get in touch with me so we can see how I can help their people.

5) Put a book review on Amazon. The more comments there are on Amazon the more likely people are to consider the book (and check it out for themselves). I would be very grateful and appreciate it, if you would do this. I thank you in advance.

6) Also, you could buy this book as a present for family, friends, colleagues and anyone you know. Not only is this a great present everyone will appreciate, it solves the problem of what to buy people for birthdays, Christmas, anniversaries, engagements, weddings, births, Hanukkah, Mother's Day, Father's Day, Valentine's Day, retirement, congratulations, prizes, to say thank you; expressions of love or friendship; expressions of gratitude or appreciation; or just because...

Finally, and in conclusion, may I thank you for reading and using this book, and may I wish you a life of much confidence, much courage, much peace, much self-esteem, much self-control, much responsibility, much fun, much happiness, much love, much appreciation, and much enjoyment.

Printed in Great Britain
by Amazon

54102428R00054